Care Bears Collectibles

An Unauthorized Handbook
and Price Guide

Jan Lindenberger

4880 Lower Valley Road, Atglen, PA 19310 USA

Copyright © 1997 by Jan Lindenberger
Library of Congress Catalog Card
    Number: 97-65939

All rights reserved. No part of this work may be reproduced or used in any form or by any means--graphic, electronic, or mechanical, including photocopying or information storage and retrieval systems--without written permission from the copyright holder.

Designed by Laurie A. Smucker

ISBN: 0-7643-0310-4
Printed in China

Published by Schiffer Publishing Ltd.
4880 Lower Valley Road
Atglen, PA 19310
Phone: (610) 593-1777
Fax: (610) 593-2002
E-mail: schifferbk@aol.com
Please contact us for a free catalog.
This book may be purchased
from the publisher.
Please include $2.95 for shipping.
Try your bookstore first.

We are interested in hearing from authors with book ideas on related subjects.

Title Page Photo:
Plush Baby Hugs and Baby Tugs. 16". $10-15 each, rare

CONTENTS

Cheer Bear sitting figurine. Friend Bear sitting on a cloud figurine. $6-10 each

Acknowledgments

A special thank you to Darlene and Walter Merian from Littleton, Colorado for opening up their home and allowing me to photograph their vast and impressive collection of Care Bears. Darlene's knowledge and excitement over her collection inspired me to do this much needed book. Thanks Darlene, for the long hours of arranging and re-arranging that special room! And especially for the fun time and laughs we had doing it and not to forget that great pizza.

Also thanks to Jo Bemis from Colorado Springs for her encouragement, her introduction to other collectors, and for sharing her collection of those wonderful Care Bears. Jo has a shop at the Colorado Springs, Colorado, Weekend Flea Market. She specializes in a nice selection of Care Bears and collectible character items.

Joel Martone of Colorado Springs, Colorado, whose shop is "Rhyme or Reason" carries a wide selection of Care Bears, along with many other character collectibles provided much assistance. Many thanks Joel.

Thanks also to Jill Stovall of Colorado Springs, Colorado for allowing me to bring her collection to my studio to photograph for this book.

The best part of putting this book together were the wonderful new friends I have made. Thanks again to all who participated and made this much needed Care Bears information and price guide possible.

Alexis Nicole Moore with Cheer Bear and Tenderheart Bear. 36". $95-125 each. Alexis is the granddaughter of Darlene and Walter Merian. Darlene started her collection for Alexis, when Alexis was a little girl, taking her from shop to shop on her hunt. Now both Alexis and Darlene are avid collectors and lovers of the Care Bears.

Introduction

As the Care Bears package says, "High above the clouds and rainbows is a place called CARE-A-LOT, which is the home of the Care Bears. There's a very special place down the rainbow river called FOREST OF FEELINGS, where the Care Bear Cousins live. Each one of the Care Bears and the Care Bear Cousins have a unique tummy symbol, describing a different personality trait, to always help you to do your very best. These special bears love to be cuddled and hugged." This description captures these cute characters and gives a clue as to why they so inspire the imagination and affections of millions of people.

The plush Care Bears came in 13" and 18", Grams Bear 15", and the Cousins were 13". All were washable. (Some of the sizes of the Bears in this guide may differ due to washing and drying.)

From 1982 through 1984 Kenner Products made Care Bears figurines which were rubber and poseable. They were distributed by American Greetings. There were thirteen Bears. Each bear measures approximately 3.5" and had a tiny tuft of hair on the top of their head. The names of the bears are Tenderheart Bear, Bedtime Bear, Birthday Bear, Cheer Bear, Grumpy Bear, Friend Bear, Love-a-Lot Bear, Wish Bear, Funshine Bear, Good Luck Bear, Baby Hugs Bear, Baby Tugs Bear, and Grams Bear. Professor Cold Heart and the Cloudkeeper completed the group. In 1985 two more bears joined the family, Share Bear and Champ Bear.

Newer Plush Cheer Bear, Tenderheart Bear, and Love-a-Lot Bear. 1991. $5-10

These figures were sold separately from 1982-84. Their play pieces were added in 1985. Birthday Bear held a Birthday Banner. Wish Bear came with a Star-Scoop, Grumpy Bear with Dumbrellas, Cheer Bear with a Merry Megaphone, and Bedtime Bear with a Snooze Alarm. Tenderheart Bear was supplied with a Caring Heart Mirror, Love-a-Lots with a Bouquet of Hearts, and Share Bear with Share-Alike Shake. Friend Bear had a Friendly Sprinkler, Champ Bear a Good Sport Trophy, and Good Luck Bear a Happy-Go-Lucky Shovel. Funshine Bear was equipped with a Star Catcher, Baby Tugs Bear had Big Diggity Bucket, Baby Hugs Bear had a Sweet Lickity Lollipop. Grams Bear had a Lovin' Basket. Professor Cold Heart had a Frozen Meanie Mug, and Cloudkeeper a Fluffy Cloud Broom.

Care Bear Cousins were also rubber/vinyl and poseable. They also joined the family in 1985. These Cousins also measured approximately 3.5" and had their own separate play pieces. Brave Heart Lion had a Trusty Shield, Cozy Heart Penguin had N'Ice Skates, and Swift Heart Rabbit had a Speedy Skateboard. Bright Heart Raccoon came with Clever Candle, Gentle Heart Lamb with Peek-A-Boo Bell, and Lotsa Heart Elephant with Mighty Trunk.

The full set of Cousins included Cozy Heart Penguin, Lotsa Heart Elephant, Bright Heart Raccoon, Playful Heart Monkey, Proud Heart Cat, Gentle Heart Lamb, Treat Heart Pig, Loyal Heart Dog, Brave Heart Lion, Swift Heart Rabbit.

Please take this book with you on your hunt for those elusive Bears and their Cousins. I hope you find it helpful in identifying and pricing these very collectible Care Bears, toys, and accessories. Remember, prices may vary according to area as well as demand, availability and condition.

Wooden Care Bear Cousins puzzles. Brave Heart Lion and Bright Heart Raccoon. $15-20 each

Figurines

PVC

PVC figurines. Baby Tugs with blocks, rare. Baby Hugs with paper dolls, rare. Grumpy Bear with Dumbrella, Wish Bear with wish bone, Bedtime Bear with blanket. 2". $8-15 each.

PVC figurines. Grumpy Bear with fallen ice cream, Funshine Bear with heart, Cheer Bear with magic lamp, Baby Hugs Bear with ball, Grumpy Bear with spilled paint. 2". $8-15 each

PVC figurines. Cheer Bear with megaphone, Friend Bear with Popsicle, Cheer Bear with paintbrush, Love-a-lot Bear with basket of hearts, Friend Bear with ice cream soda. 2". $8-15 each

PVC figurines. Birthday Bear with bottle, Birthday Bear wearing hat and holding baby bottle, Birthday Bear with present, Funshine Bear with baton, Funshine Bear with bird on shoulder. 2". $8-15 each

PVC figurines. Share Bear with hearts, Tenderheart Bear hugging, Grams Bear, Friend Bear with flower, Tenderheart Bear with star. 2". $8-15 each

Hugging Tenderheart, Friend Bear holding flower, and Friend Bear holding popsicle. $8-15

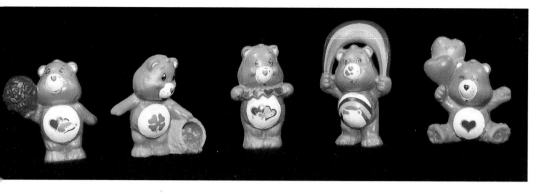

Love-a-lot with flowers, Good Luck with basket, Love-a-lot holding hearts, Cheer Bear holding rainbow, Tenderheart holding balloon hearts. $8-15

Mini Bedtime Bear with night cap, Baby Tugs with shovel and pail, Good Luck Bear with horse shoe. Good Luck with cap, and Cheer Bear as an artist. $8-15

PVC figurines. Bedtime Bear and Wish Bear laying on clouds. 3". $8-15 each

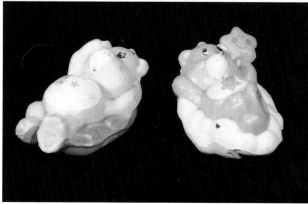

Rubber Tenderheart Bear figurine in package. 3.5". $15-20

Ceramic

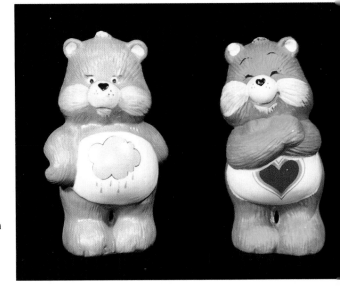

Ceramic Grumpy Bear and
Tenderheart Bear. $7-14 each

Ceramic Cheer Bear using the
telephone. 2.5" X 3". $7-14

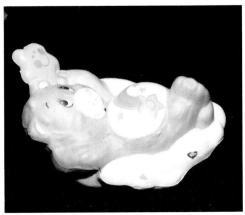

Ceramic Wish Bear laying on a
cloud. $7-14

Care Bear Cousins ceramic figurines. $7-14 each

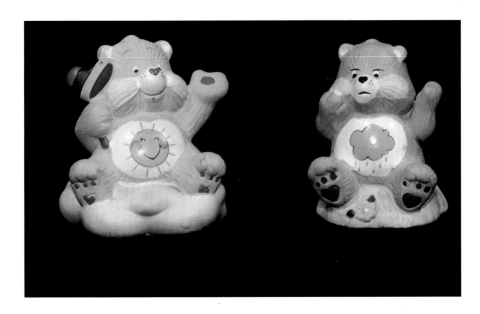

Ceramic Funshine Bear figurine sitting on a cloud. Grumpy Bear sitting on grass. $7-14

Ceramic Grumpy Bear, Funshine Bear, Good Luck Bear, Tenderheart Bear and Wish Bear figurines. $7-14 each

Ceramic Bedtime Bear, Love-a-Lot Bear, Birthday Bear and Cheer Bear figurines. $7-14

Ceramic Lotsa Heart Elephant Cousin figurine. $7-14

Ceramic Love-a-lot Bear figurine. $7-14

Ceramic figurines. Friend Bear, Grumpy Bear, Bedtime Bear, Good Luck Bear, Tenderheart Bear, Funshine Bear. $7-14 each

Rubber

Rubber poseable Good Luck Bear and Grams Bear in original packages. 3.5". $8-15

Rubber poseable Birthday Bear and Wish Bear in original packages. 3.5". $8-15

Funshine Bear and Wish Bear poseable figurines in original packages. 3.5". $8-15

Rubber poseable Bright Heart Raccoon with Clever Candle and Baby Hugs Bear with Sweet Lickity Lollipop. $15-20 each

Rubber poseable Brave Heart Lion with trusty shield. Care Bear Cousin. 3.5". $20-25

Rubber poseable Grumpy Bear and Bedtime Bear boxed. $8-15 each

Rubber poseable Funshine Bear, Birthday Bear, Wish Bear, Cheer Bear. 3.5". $6-10

Rubber poseable Good Luck Bear, Friend Bear, Love-a- lot Bear, Champ Bear. 3.5". $6-10

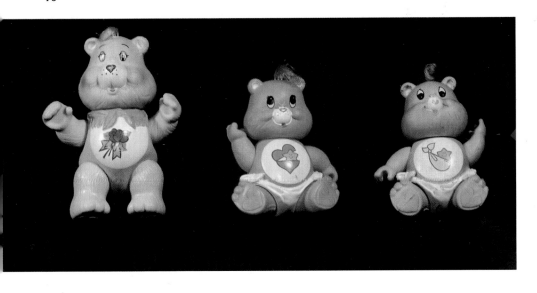

Rubber Grams Bear, Baby Hugs and Baby Tugs poseable bears. 3.5". $6-10 each

PVC figures of the Cloudkeeper. 2.5". $10-15. Rubber poseable Cloudkeeper. 4". $15-20 rare

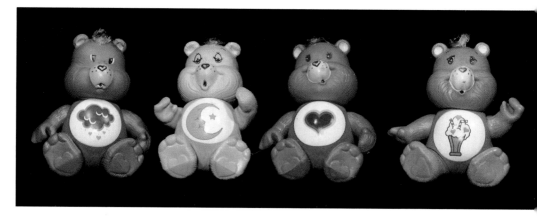

Rubber poseable Care Bears. Grumpy Bear, Bedtime Bear, Tenderheart Bear, Share Bear. $6-10 each

Rubber, poseable Care Bear Cousins. Cozy Heart Penguin, Gentle Heart Lamb, Lotsa Heart Elephant, Brave Heart Lion, Bright Heart Raccoon, Swift Heart Rabbit. 3.5". $8-15 each, rare

Rubber poseable Funshine Bear with Star Catcher. 3.5". $10-15

Rubber poseable Tenderheart Bear with Caring Heart Mirror. 3.5". $10-15

PVC figure of Professor Cold Heart. 3.5". $10-15. Rubber poseable Professor Cold Heart. 3.5". $15-20 rare

Rubber poseable Cheer Bear with Merry Megaphone. 3.5". $10-15

Rubber poseable Birthday Bear with Happy Birthday Banner. 3.5". $15-20

Rubber poseable Baby Tugs with Big Diggity Bucket. 3.5". $20-25 Rare

Rubber poseable Cozy Heart Penguin with N'ice Skates. Care Bear Cousin. 3.5". $20-25. Rare

Plush Bears

Plush Share Bear, Grumpy Bear,
Tenderheart Bear. 16". $10-15 each

Plush Cheer Bear. 36". $150-200

Plush Grams Bear. 14". $30-40. Rare

Plush Birthday Bear, Love-A-Lot Bear and Bedtime Bear. 16". $10-15

Plush Funshine Bear, Cheer Bear and Wish Bear. 16". $10-15

Plush Champ Bear, Good Luck Bear and Friend Bear. 16". $10-15 each

Plush Brave Heart Lion, Lotsa Heart Elephant. 16". $15-20 each

Plush Bright Heart Raccoon and Gentle Heart Lamb. 16". $15-20 each

Plush talking Secret Bear. 1983. 16". $40-50

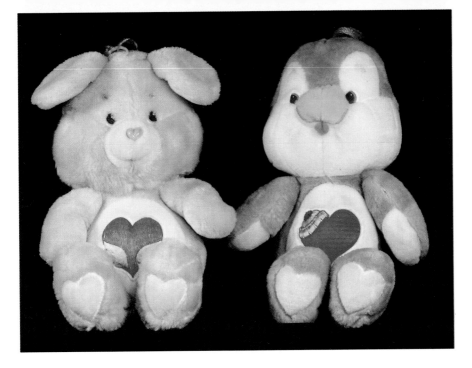

Plush Swift Heart Rabbit and Cozy Heart Penguin. 16". $15-20 each

Plush Love-a-Lot and Birthday Bears. 16". $10-15

Plush hard face Chubby with velour face Cousins Bright Heart Raccoon and Swift Heart Rabbit, and Funshine Bear. 11". 1986. $20-30

Satin, stuffed Friend Bear. Rare. $25-35

Plush hard face Chubby Tenderheart Bear, Cheer Bear, and Bedtime Bear. Velour faces. 11". 1986. $20-30

Plush Tenderheart and Cheer Bears. 16". $10-15

Plush Good Luck and Bedtime Bears. 16". $10-15

Plush Mini Grumpy Bear, Good Luck Bear, and Funshine Bear. Original tags. Rare. $30-40

Plush Mini Champ Bear (top), Share Bear, Cheer Bear, Friend Bear, and Birthday Bear. Rare. $30-40

Plush Mini Love-a-Lot Bear, Bedtime Bear, Wish Bear, and Tenderheart Bear. Rare. $30-40

Plush Bedtime Bear and Tenderheart Bear, 1991. Note change in hair tuft. $5-$10

Newer Plush Tree Planting Bear and 4th of July Bear. 1991. $5-10

Pillow Dolls

Cotton stuffed pillows, Brave Heart Lion, Lotsa-Heart Elephant. $15-20

Cotton stuffed pillow Swift Heart Rabbit. $15-20

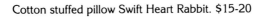

Cotton stuffed Cheer Bear pillow. $15-20

Cotton stuffed Wish Bear pillow. $15-20

Cotton stuffed pillow Birthday Bear, Friend Bear, and Love-a-Lot Bear. $15-20

Cotton stuffed Funshine Bear, Good luck Bear, Tenderheart Bear, and Grumpy Bear pillows. $15-20 each

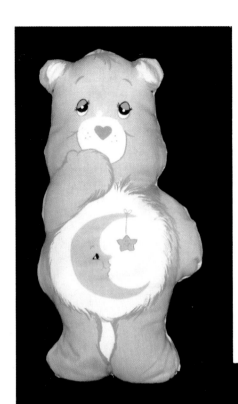

Cotton stuffed Bedtime Bear pillow.
$15-20

Cotton stuffed Friend Bear pillow.
$10-15

Cotton stuffed Baby Hugs, Grams, and Baby Tugs pillows. $20-30 each. Rare.

Cotton stuffed Care Bear Cousins pillows. Bright Heart Raccoon, Gentle Heart Lamb, Cozy Heart Penguin. $15-20

Cotton stuffed pillows, Treat Heart Pig and Proud Heart Cat. $15-20

Cotton stuffed pillow, Playful Heart Monkey and Loyal Heart Dog. $15-20

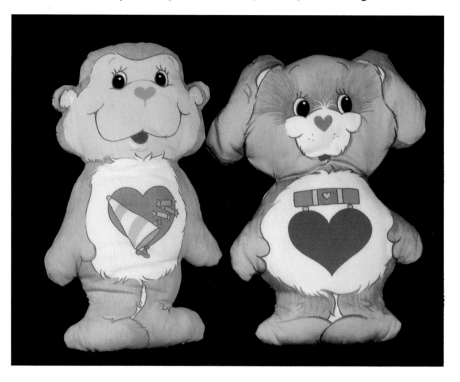

Uncut cotton pillows. Playful Heart Monkey and Loyal Heart Dog, Care Bear Cousins. $10-15

Uncut cotton Funshine Bear and Wish Bear pillows. $10-15

Uncut cotton pillows. Gentle Heart Lamb and Brave Heart Lion, Care Bear Cousins. $10-15

Uncut cotton Cheer Bear and Good Luck Bear pillows. $10-15

Uncut cotton Birthday Bear and Tenderheart Bear pillow. $10-15

Butterick patterns for Friend Bear, Grams Bear, and Cheer Bear. $15-20 each

Butterick patterns for Bedtime Bear, Grumpy Bear, Baby Hugs and Baby Tugs. $15-20 each

Butterick Care Bears pattern. $15-20   Butterick Care Bears craft pattern. $15-20

Large cotton stuffed pillow Cheer Bear. $50-65

Kitchen

Metal Care Bears serving tray. "Here come the bears!" $9-14

Metal child's serving tray. $9-14

Metal Care Bear Cousins serving tray. "Make way for the cousins!" $9-14

Hard board Care Bears toy sink. $65-85

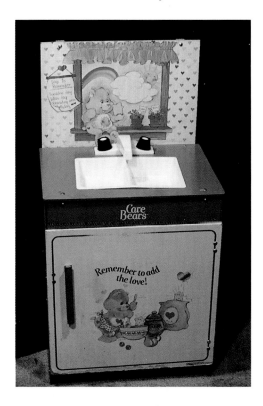

Care Bears Cookie Bake Set. $30-45

Ceramic trivet. $6-10

Cotton Care Bears apron and pot holders. $35-45 set

Birthday Bear Stand-up Cake Pan Set from Wilton. $15-20

Care Bears and Cousins magnets. $3-6 each

Aluminum Birthday Bear cake pan from Wilton. Plastic decoration with Birthday Bear. $10-15

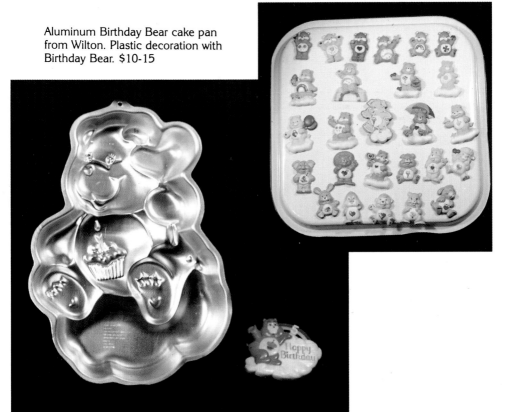

Ceramic Cheer Bear cookie jar. $85-125

Ceramic Funshine Bear cookie jar. $85-125

Share Bear drinking glass. $6-10

Bedtime Bear juice glass. $8-12

Glass bowls and juice glasses. $40-50 set

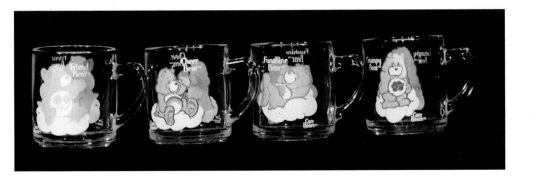

Glass cups. Friend Bear, Cheer Bear, Funshine Bear, and Grumpy Bear. $7-10 each

Glasses from Pizza Hut. Cheer Bear, Grumpy Bear, Tenderheart Bear, and Funshine Bear. $7-10 each

Ceramic Care Bears cups. Name inside cup. $15-25 each

Ceramic cups. Gentle Heart Lamb, Lotsa Heart Elephant, and Love-a-Lot Bear. $7-10 each

Ceramic cup. Birthday Bear. Birthday #1. $10-15

Ceramic cups. Wish Bear, Tenderheart Bear, and Brave Heart Lion with Gentle Heart Lamb. $7-10 each

Ceramic cups. Birthday Bear, Tenderheart Bear, and Funshine Bear. $7-10 each

Ceramic cups. Good Luck Bear, Tenderheart Bear, and Love-a-Lot Bear. $7-10 each

Ceramic cups. Wish Bear, Share Bear, and Cheer Bear. $7-10 each

Porcelain decorator plates. $15-25 each

Plastic Wish Bear cup and glass. $4-6 each

Lotsa Heart Elephant plastic note pad. $10-15

Plastic Care Bear Cousins drinking cups. $6-10 each

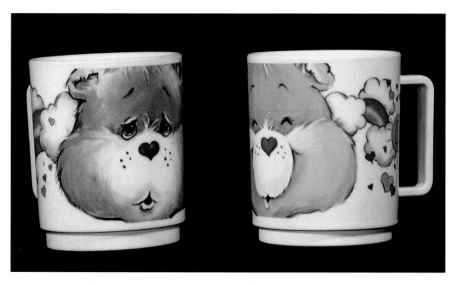

Plastic drinking cups with Care Bear heads. $6-10 each

Plastic drinking cups. Bears wearing hats. $8-12 each

Gummi Bear products with Care Bears. $10-15 set

Plastic Care Bears cup. $5-8

Plastic cereal/soup bowl. $6-10

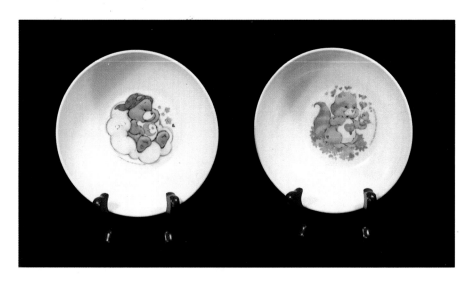

Plastic Bedtime Bear and Bright Heart Raccoon bowls. $6-10 each

Plastic Love-a-Lot Bear cereal bowl. $6-10

Plastic cup from Pizza Hut. $7-10

Plastic Care Bear Cousins plate. $8-15

51

Plastic bucket filled with Pierre's cookies. $6-10

Plastic divided dish. $8-15

Plastic Care Bears plate with Wish
Bear and Love-a-Lot Bear. $8-15

Front and back of plastic placemat. $5-8

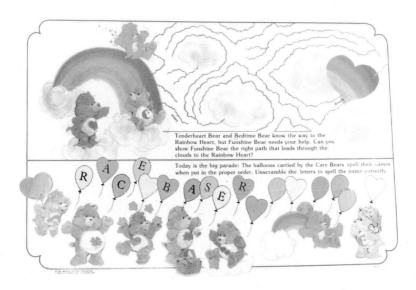

Front and back of plastic placemat. $5-8

Clocks, Radios, Lamps, and Banks

Plastic quartz alarm clock from Bradley. $45-55

Resin clock with Friend Bear sitting on top. $30-40

Plastic quartz alarm clock from Bradley. $45-55

Metal Care Bears alarm clock. $45-55

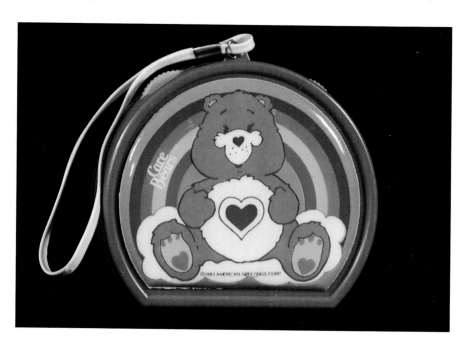

Plastic Tenderheart Bear radio. $40-50

Cotton hanging wall clock. $20-30

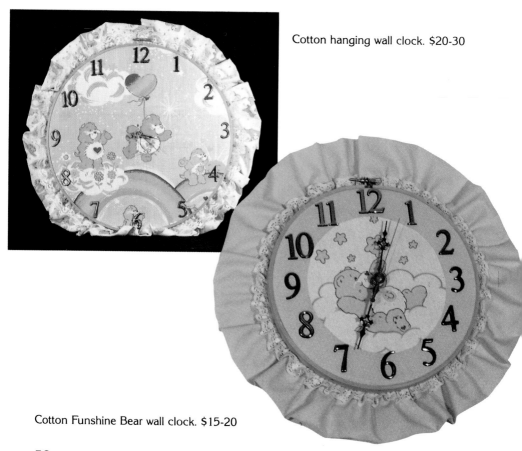

Cotton Funshine Bear wall clock. $15-20

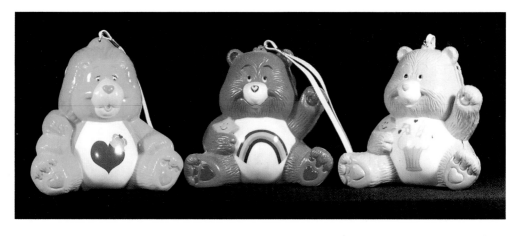

Plastic Tenderheart Bear, Cheer Bear, and Share Bear radios. 6". $30-40 each

Plastic tape players. $30-40 each

Plastic Tenderheart Bear radios. $35-45

Plastic Care Bears lamp. $35-45

Care Bears cassette tape recorder. $50-60

Plastic Care Bears phonograph with original box. $60-75

Ceramic Bedtime Bear lamp with cardboard shade. $35-50

Ceramic Baby Hugs and Baby Tugs lamp. $30-45

Bedtime Care Bears plastic night light. $40-50

Ceramic Bedtime Bear lamp with cardboard shade. $35-50

Plastic Bedtime Bear night light. $8-12

Funshine Bear night light. 4.5". $15-20

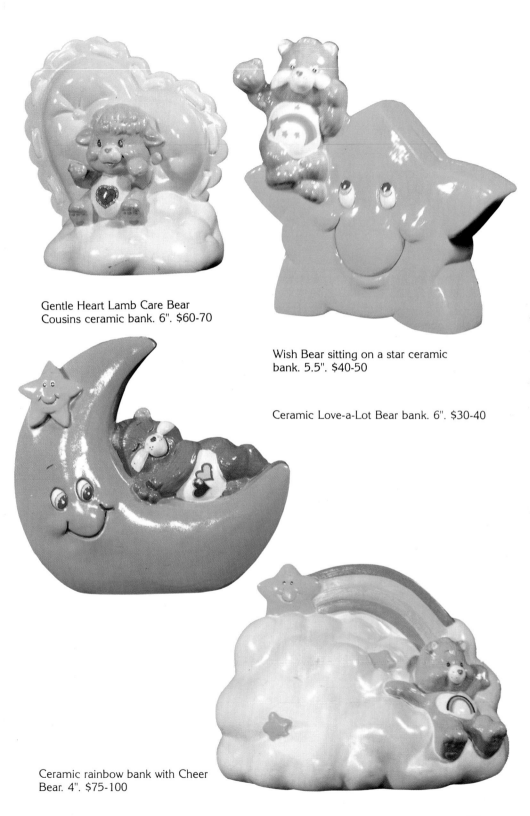

Gentle Heart Lamb Care Bear
Cousins ceramic bank. 6". $60-70

Wish Bear sitting on a star ceramic
bank. 5.5". $40-50

Ceramic Love-a-Lot Bear bank. 6". $30-40

Ceramic rainbow bank with Cheer
Bear. 4". $75-100

Ceramic banks. "For rainbow days" and "Spread a little happiness around." 3.5". $30-40

Ceramic banks. "The nicest things happen when friends get together" and "A friend is someone you can count on." 4". $30-40 each

Plush Funshine Bear and Tenderheart Bear banks. 8". $30-40 each

Plush Birthday Bear and Love-a-Lot Bear banks. 8". $30-40 each

Plush Wish Bear and Cheer Bear banks. 8". $30-40 each

Ceramic banks. Treat Heart Pig, Bright Heart Raccoon, Proud Heart Cat. 6". $35-45

63

Funshine Bear with blue bird, plastic music box. 5". $50-75

Cheer Bear bank. Rubber/vinyl. 8". $35-45

Ceramic music box. Love-a-Lot Bear in the clouds. 8.5 ". $75-100

Plastic Love-a-Lot Bear music box. 5.5". $50-75

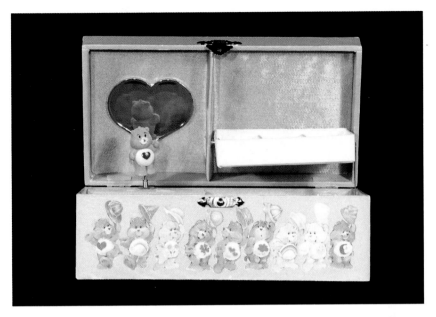

Cardboard music box. Tenderheart Bear twirls around. $40-55

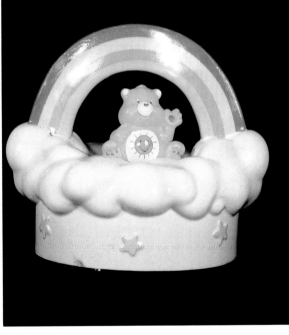

Ceramic Cheer Bear musical rocking chair. $35-45

Ceramic Funshine Bear sitting on a cloud, music box. 6". $60-75

Schooltime

Metal Care Bear Cousins lunch box with thermos. $30-40

Metal Care Bears lunch box with thermos. $30-40

Plastic lunch box with thermos. $15-25

Plastic lunch box with thermos. $15-25

Plastic lunch box with thermos. $15-25

Plastic lunch box with thermos. $15-25

Plastic lunch box with thermos. $15-25

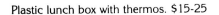
Plastic lunch box with thermos. $15-25

Plastic lunch box with thermos. $15-25

Plastic lunch box with thermos. $15-25

Plastic lunch box with thermos. $15-25

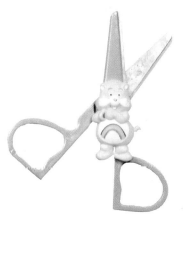

Funshine Bear paper holder/folder. $4-6

Plastic Cheer Bear scissors. $6-10

Tenderheart and Love-a-Lot Bear note books. $6-10

Love-a-Lot Bear and Cheer Bear paper holders/folders. $4-6 each

Care Bear Cousins cardboard paper holder/folder. $4-6 each

Wooden magnetic play desk with
plastic seat. Care Bears design on
back of chair. $75-100

Containers

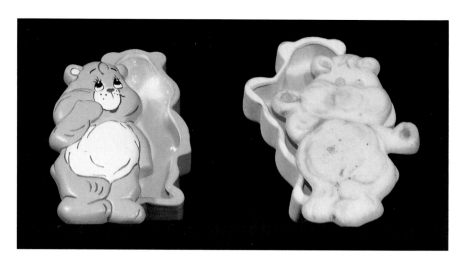

Ceramic Care Bears jewelry boxes. $15-20 each

Friend Bear and Funshine Bear trinket boxes. $7-12 each

Ceramic trinket box with Funshine Bear sitting on top. $15-20

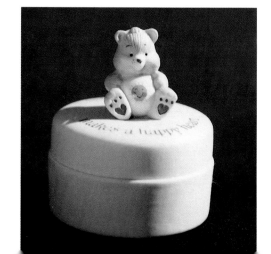

Metal "treat" can. $6-10

Metal holiday tin with Bedtime Bear and Good Luck Bear. $6-10

Metal Care Bear Cousins and Care Bears trinket boxes. $8-12 each

Tin Care Bears containers. $6-10 each

Tin Care Bears containers. $6-10 each

Tin cookie can. $8-12

Metal waste paper can. $20-30

Metal waste paper can. $20-30

Wall Hangings and Pictures

Wooden wall plaques. $12-18 each

Plaster Funshine Bear plaque. $6-10

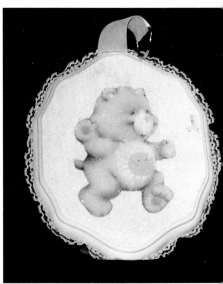

Plaster Champ Bear wall plaque. $6-10

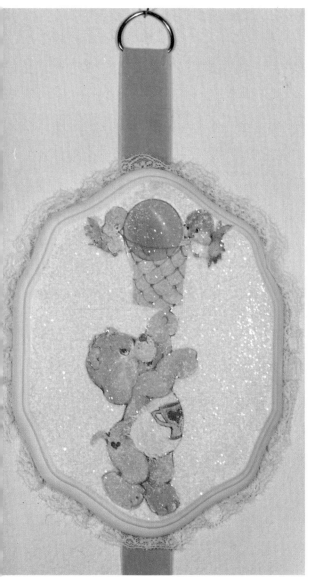

Plaster Tenderheart Bear and Cheer
Bear wall plaque. $6-10

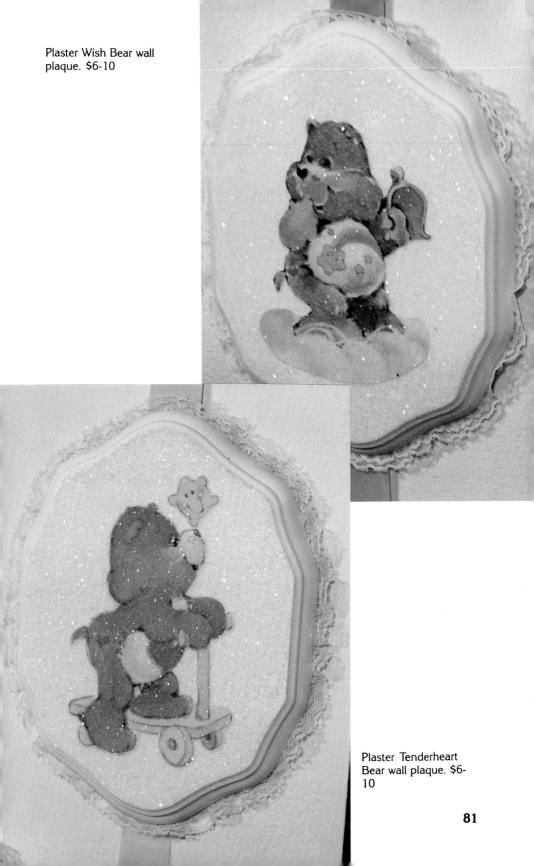

Plaster Wish Bear wall plaque. $6-10

Plaster Tenderheart Bear wall plaque. $6-10

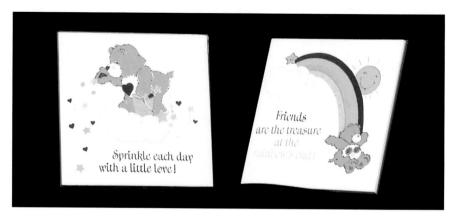

Ceramic Care Bears trivets. $6-10 each

Ceramic Birthday Bear picture frame. $10-15

Plastic framed Tenderheart and Friend Bear pictures. $8-15 each

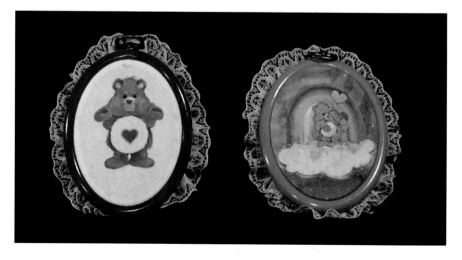

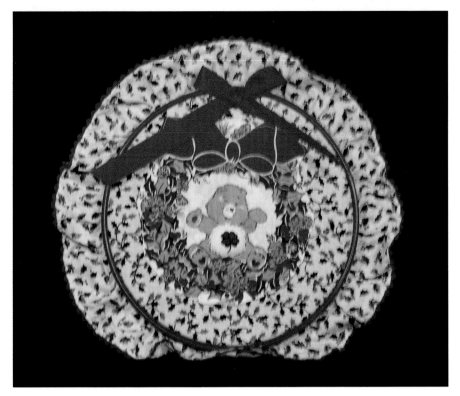

Cotton Good Luck Bear wall hanging. $5-8

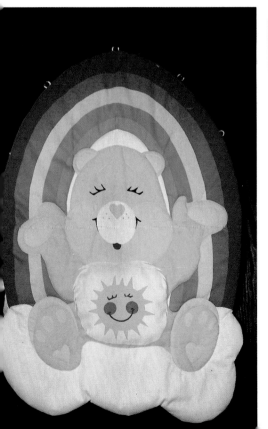

Glass Funshine Bear picture. $10-15

Funshine Bear cotton wall hanging.
34". $35-45

83

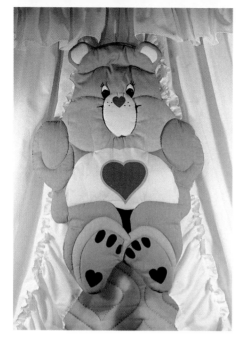

Cotton Tenderheart Bear wall
hanging. 29". $35-45

The box for Cheer Bear Soft
Stitches. 29". $15-20

Cardboard grow chart. $10-15

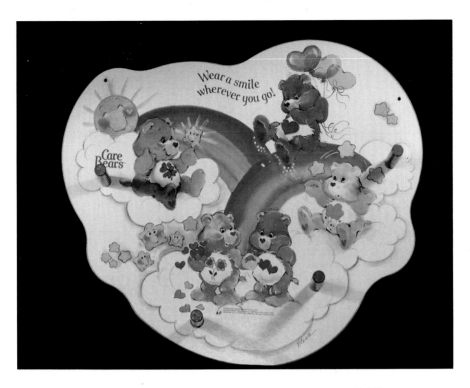

Care Bears wall hanging clothes rack. Hard board. $40-55

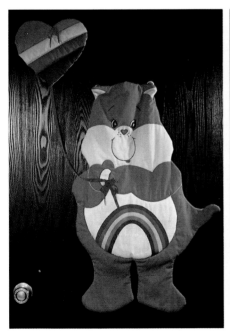

Cotton Cheer Bear wall hanging. 29".
$35-45

Wooden wall plaque from Designers
Collection. American Greeting Cards.
$6-8

Cotton poster of Bedtime Bear. 17" x 25". $15-20

Cotton poster of Friend Bear. 17" x 25". $15-20

Purses and Totes

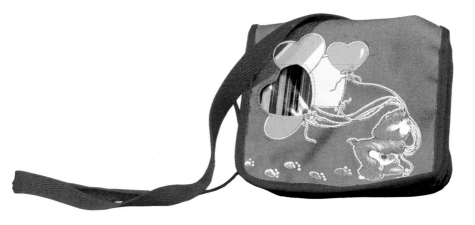

Child's Love-a-Lot Bear vinyl purse. $8-10

Fabric Care Bears wallet with
Tenderheart and Cheer Bears. $10-
15

Cheer Bear child's cotton "Funtime"
tote bag. $10-15

Tenderheart Bear vinyl heart-shaped child's purse. $8-10

Tenderheart and Cheer Bears child's
vinyl playtime purse. $8-10

Vinyl child's purse. $10-15

Vinyl Tote bags. Tenderheart Bear and Cheer Bear. $8-10

Vinyl Friend Bear heart-shaped child's purse. $8-10

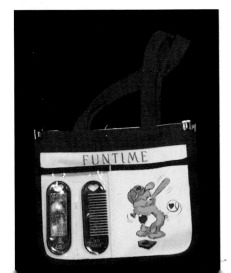

Vinyl "Funtime" purse with comb and mirror. $10-15

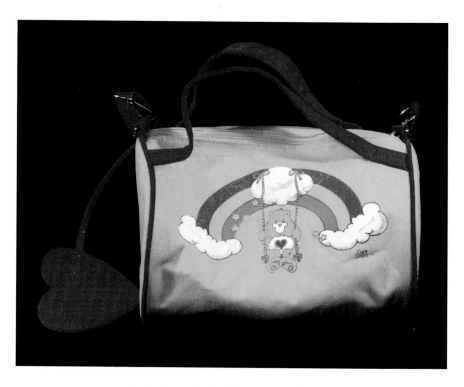

Tenderheart vinyl child's tote bag. $10-15

Cheer Bear and Love-a-Lot Bear child's vinyl school bag. $10-15

Fabric tote bag with Good Luck Bear,
Friend Bear, Love-a-Lot Bear,
Grumpy Bear, and Tenderheart Bear.
$10-15

Fabric tote bag with Wish Bear,
Funshine Bear, Cheer Bear, and
Grumpy Bear. $10-15

Fabric tote bag with Friend Bear
sitting on a cloud. $10-15

"Smile" Care Bears vinyl tote bag. $10-15

Fabric "Love" tote bag. $8-15

Cheer Bear and Love-a-Lot child's vinyl tote bag. $10-15

Fabric duffle bag with Love-a-Lot Bear and Good luck Bear. "You never know where you'll find a friend." $10-15

Vinyl "Here comes fun!" child's purse. $10-15

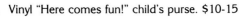

Plastic child's gym bag. $15-20

Fabric carrying case. "Wherever you go whatever you do be sure to take a smile with you!" $10-15

Yellow fabric carrying case with Cheer Bear and Funshine Bear. "Getting there is half the fun!" $10-15

Fabric carrying case. "Setting sail for grandmas." 1986. $10-15

Black fabric carrying case with Cheer Bear and Funshine Bear. "Getting there is half the fun!" $10-15

Red fabric carrying case with Cheer Bear and Funshine Bear. "Getting there is half the fun". $10-15

Plastic Wish Bear back pack. $15-20

Vinyl pencil bag. $6-8

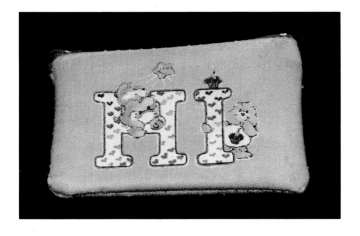

Party Time

Money Christmas card. $4-6

Care Bears greeting cards. $5-7 each

Box of Greeting cards. $4-6

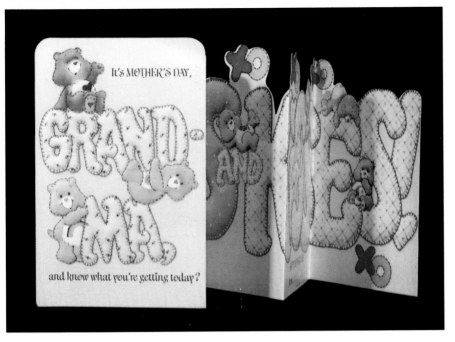

Care Bears greeting card. $5-7

Valentine's day cards. $4-6

Greeting card. $4-6   Greeting card. $4-6

Thanksgiving greeting card. $4-6

Tri-fold greeting card. $4-6

Christmas cards, self-mailing with stickers. $15-20

Care Bears greeting cards. $15-20

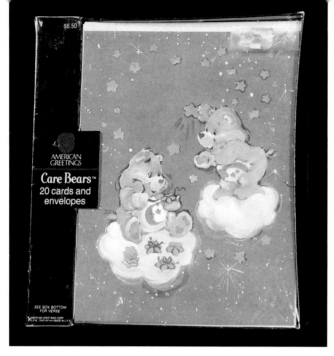

Greeting cards with envelopes. $15-20

Christmas cards with envelopes. $15-20

Care Bears pop-up greeting cards. $15-20

Christmas cards with matching envelopes. $15-20

"Let the fun shine in!" greeting cards. $10-15

Two packs of party invitations. $6-10 each

Boxed valentines. $10-15

Boxed Valentines. $10-15

Boxed valentines. $10-15

Five packages of party invitations. $6-10 each

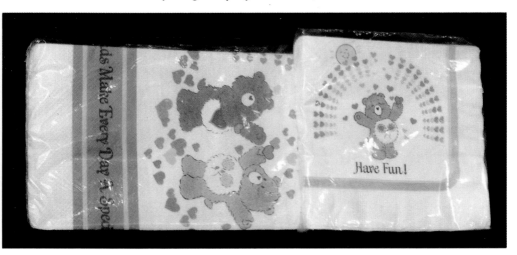

Party paper napkins and table cover. $10-15

Paper party napkins. $6-10 each pack

Paper birthday party table cover. $10-18

Plastic birthday party table cover. $10-18

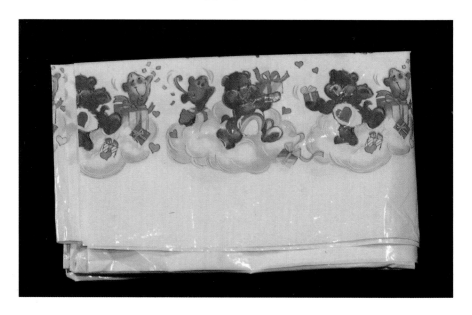

Paper birthday party table cover. $10-18

Paper birthday party table cover. $10-18

Plastic party bags. $8-12

Paper party pack. $15-20

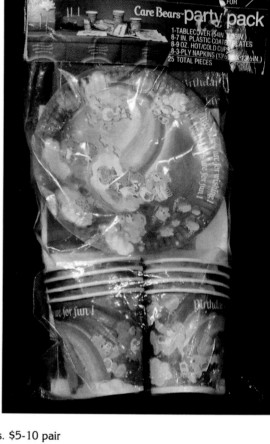

Set of four paper birthday hats and horns. $5-10 pair

Care Bears holiday decoration. $10-15

Paper pull apart fanning Christmas decoration. $10- 15

Paper plates and bowls. $6-10 each

Multi-pack invitations and thank you notes. $6-10

Holiday gift labels. $7-10

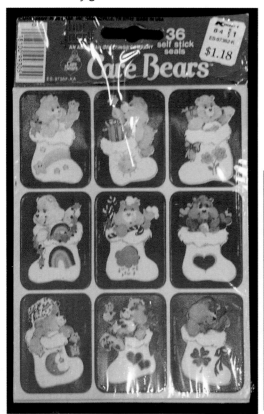

Care Bears advent calendar with envelope. $15-20

Giant gift tags, holiday stickers, gift tags. $8-12 each

Roll of gift wrapping. $8-12

Silk birthday ribbon. $7-12

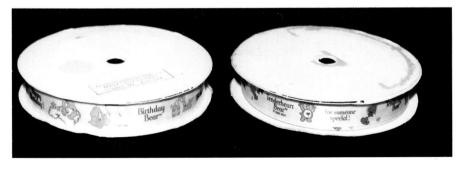

Care Bears "All-in-One" wrapping paper and bow. $10-15

Plastic Love-a-Lot Bear balloon. $7-12

Plastic Birthday Bear balloon. $7-12

112

Tenderheart Bear halloween costume. $20-30

Good Luck Bear banner. $20-30

Two packs of Care Bears stickers. $5-8 each

Cotton holiday Funshine Bear stuffed doll. $15-20

Cotton Christmas stocking. $6-10

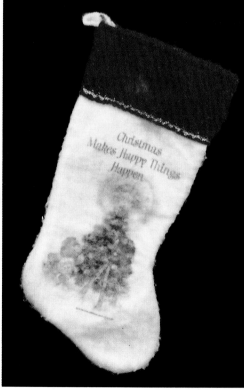

114

Punch out decorations. $6-8   "Care Bears Stamp Fun" book. $5-7

"Play it safe!" sticker book. $6-10

Presto Magix Stick 'n Lift Care Bears
from Rose Art. $10-15

"Caring and Sharing" sticker book.
$5-7

Puzzles and Games

Wooden Cheer Bear puzzle from Playtime. $15-20

Care Bears 70 piece puzzles. $6-10 each

Tenderheart Bear Valentines Day puzzle. $6-10

25 piece mini Care Bears puzzles. $5-7 each

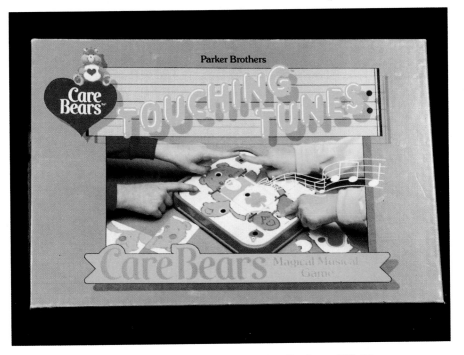

Care Bears "Touching Tunes" by Parker Brothers. $30-40

Match the blocks puzzle from Craft Master. $10-15

Funshine Bear match up card game. $8-15

Care Bears card games. "Which bears where?" "Spell bear." "How many bears?" $5-10 each

Care Bears puzzle set. $5-8 each

Care Bears record player. $40-55

"Care-a-Lot" and "Warm Feelings" games. $10-15 each

Records, Tapes, and Videos

Record, "The Care Bears Off to See the World." $15-20

Record, "The Care Bears Birthday Party." $15-20

Record, "The Care Bears Christmas." $15-20

Record, "The Care Bears Adventures in Care-a-Lot." $20-30 rare

Record, "The Care Bears Movie."
Original sound track. Kid Stuff
Records. $20-30

Plastic record with imprinted Care
Bears on the disc. "Love Is All
Around." $15-20

Record, "The Care Bears Adventures
in Care-a-Lot." Kid Stuff Records.
$15-20

Record, "The Care Bears Care for
You." Kid Stuff Records. $15-20

123

"See, Hear and Read" records included books. $7-12 each

"See, Hear and Read" records with books. $7-12 each

"Care Bears Bedtime Story" and "Meet the Care Bears" records. $7-12 each

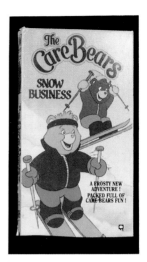

Care Bears video: "Snow Business." $15-20

"The Care Bears Battle the Freeze Machine," packaging variation. $15-20

Record, "The Care Bears Adventures in Care-a-Lot." $20-30 rare

Cardboard Care Bears Record Tote. $20-30

125

"See, Hear and Read" book and record combinations. "12 Days of Christmas" and "The Care Bears' Picnic." $7-12

Care Bears videos: "Care Bears, The Magic Shop & Concrete Rain;" "Great moments in Caring," In Space: First Stage." $15-20 each

Care Bears videos: "Be My Valentine," "The Clan of the Care Bears," "The Care Bears Music Video." $15-20 each

Care Bears videos: "Rainy Day Activities," "The Care Bears Meet the Lovable Monsters," "The Care Bears Battle the Freeze Machine." $15-25 each

Care Bears videos: "Timeless Tales," "Feeling Good," "In the Land Without Feelings." $15-25 each

Care Bears videos: "Soap Box Derby," "Save the Day!" "Braces." $15-20 each

Record, "The Care Bears Off to See the World." $15-20

Care Bears videos: "Care Bears Movie II: A New Generation," two versions of packaging; The Care Bears Family Picnic." $15-25 each

127

Books

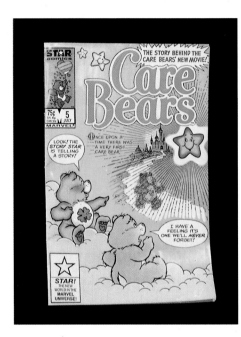

Care Bears comic from Marvel comics. $30-40

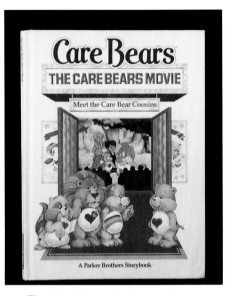

The Care Bears Movie story book. $10-15

The Care Bears' Circus of Shapes book. $10-15

Care Bear Cousins hard back books: *The Best Prize of All* and *Keep on Caring.* $10-15 each

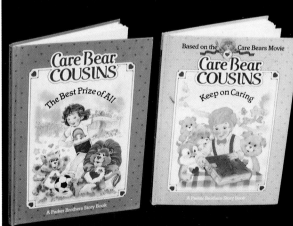

Care Bears Alphabet Book, Counting Book, and Look and Find Book. $10-15

A Tale from the Care Bears: A Friend for Francis and Ben's New Buddy. Hard back books. $10-15

A Tale from the Care Bears: Caring Is What Counts and The Trouble with Timothy. Hard back books, part of a set of 11. $10-15

The Care Bears and the Whale Tale and The Care Bears and the Terrible Twos. $6-10 each

129

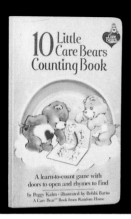

Cardboard *Wish Bear Book of Wonderful Wishes.* Random House. $8-12

10 Little Care Bears Counting Book and *Did You Ever Pet a Care Bear?* $10-15

The Care Bears' Book of Colors and *The Care Bears' Book of Feelings.* Hard back. $6-8 each

Set of seven hard cover books by Happy House Books. $40-55 set

Set of four hard back mini books.
$5-8 each

Set of four hard back books. $5-8
each

The Care Bears Birthday Party
coloring book. $10-15

The Care Bears Help Out story book. $8-12

The Care Bears & the New Baby story book. $5-8

Vinyl story book for the bath. $12-18

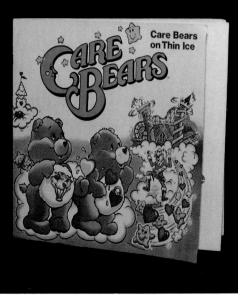

Care Bears on Thin Ice story book. $5-8

The Care Bears' Garden story book.
$7-10

*The Care Bears' Party Cookbook,
It's My Cat,* and *The Care Bear
Cousins' Mystery Adventure.* $6-10

Soft cover and hard cover, *The Care
Bears' Night Before Christmas.* $6-
10

Soft cover and hard cover, *The Care
Bears Help Santa.* $6-10

Safe and Fun Coloring Book. $6-10

133

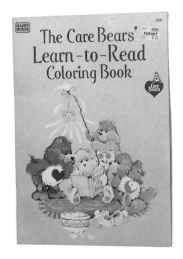

Learn-to-Read Coloring Book. $4-6

The Care Bears and the Big Sneeze,
The Care Bears Help Chase Colds,
and The Care Bear Cousins and the
Snowy Christmas. $6-10 each

Coloring and activity books. $6-10
each

Coloring books. $6-10 each

Baby and Toy Room

Gerber plastic baby bottles. $6-10

Plastic baby toy. Love-a-Lot Bear. $6-10

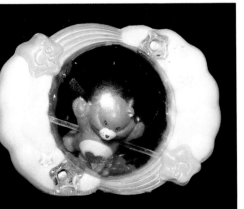

Plastic baby rattle. Tenderheart Bear. $4-8

Plastic baby rattle with unbreakable mirror. $8-12

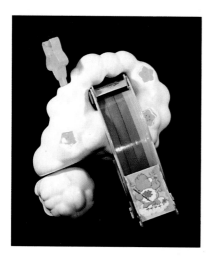

Plastic cloud with merry-go-round that pops open and Care Bears pop out. $30-40

Terry cloth stuffed Care Bears rattles with mirrors in the belly. 12". $12-20

Plastic crib hanging toy. Sunshine rotates. $15-20

Plastic Care Bears block. All sides move in different directions. $25-30

Plastic Funshine Bear BB game. BB's must go into all the holes. $10-15

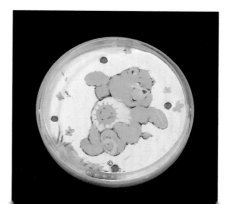

Plastic Cloud Mobile toy vehicle.
Early 1980s. $20- 25

Plastic Rainbow Roller. Early 1980s.
$25-30

Plastic Funshine Bear tambourine.
$30-40

Rubber soap dish and soap. $15-20

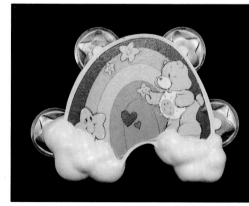

Rubber soap holder/bath squeak toy. $8-14

Plastic Care Bears play set. Set shown open and closed. Bears and furniture are removable. $60-75

Super Shaper Soap Maker. $25-35

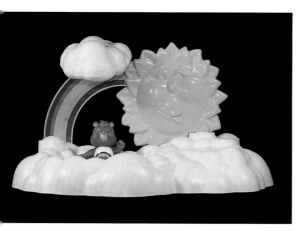

Plastic baby toy. Cheer Bear sitting on a cloud. $25-35

Plastic walkie talkie phone. They came as a pair. $40-50

Vinyl child's swim ring. $10-15

Vinyl beach ball. $8-12

Good Luck Bear rubber ball. $10-15

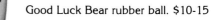

Tenderheart rubber ball. $10-15

140

Vinyl swim floater. $20-25

Vinyl swim floater. $20-25

Vinyl baby swim float. "Splash into fun." $8-15

Vinyl baby swim float in blue. $8-15

Vinyl arm floats. $6-10

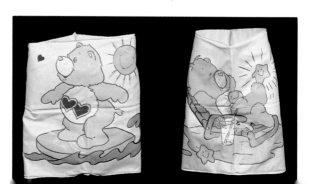

Tenderheart Bear child's ice skates with box. $30-40

Young adult's Tenderheart Bear roller skates. $30-40

Child's Tenderheart Bear roller skates. $30-40

Plastic Tenderheart Bear baby skates. $35-45

Wooden child's stool. $25-35

143

Plastic three wheeler low rider with Care Bears graphics. $50-70. Also included in this line were: a Care Bears bike with steel frame, 13", $80-100; and a plastic Roller Rider for children ages 1-3, $60-75. All these items were decorated with the Care Bears graphics.

Plastic Care Bears Sit'n Spin. Revolves with kid power. $45-60

Metal child's tricycle. $65-90

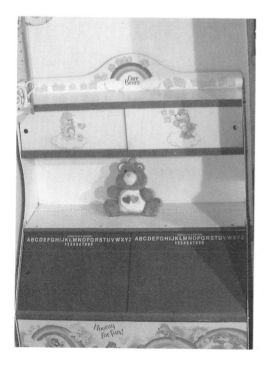

Hardboard toy box. $100-125. Included in this line (but not shown) were: a night table, 20" x 16.5" x 25", $50-65; a desk and matching chair, 22.5" x 16" x 28", $60-75; and a four-shelf bookcase, 20" x 9 x 43", $75-100. All these items were decorated with the Care Bears graphics. The Care Bear Cousins products were: an activity desk, which doubled as a toy box, with a stool, 19" x 32" x 31", $60-75; a costumer/clothes rack. 17" x 14" x 48", $50-65; and a Cousins wall clothes rack, 19.5" x 4" x 17", $30-40. The kitchen appliances were also made of hardboard. They included: the stove with a plastic hood, 16.5" x 13" x 31", $60-80; a double basin sink, 16.5" x 13 " x 31", $65-85; and a side-by-side refrigerator/freezer, 15.5" x 13" x 31", $65-85.

145

Hardboard Care Bears toy box. $50-75

Plastic baby seat/walker. $60-75

Plastic bed/play tent from Outdoor Venture Corp. $35- 45

Linens

Most of all the linen line came with matching pillow cases, curtains, sheets, sleeping bags, quilts, comforters, pillow shams, canopies. The blankets came in flannel as well as cotton. They came with the Care Bear graphics and the Care Bear Cousin graphics.

Baby quilt with ruffle and without ruffle. $35-45

Quilted cotton baby quilt. $35-45

Quilted cotton baby quilt. $35-45

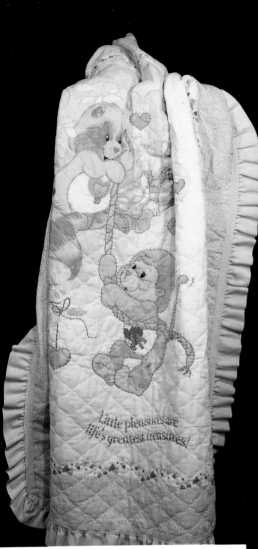

Quilted cotton baby quilt. $35-45

Little pleasures are
life's greatest treasures!

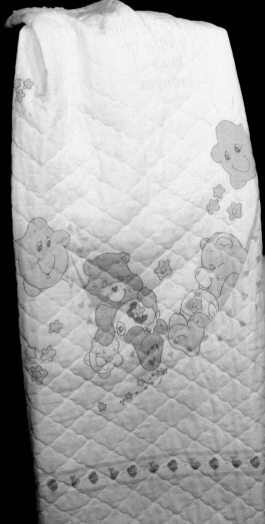

Quilted cotton baby quilt. $35-45

148

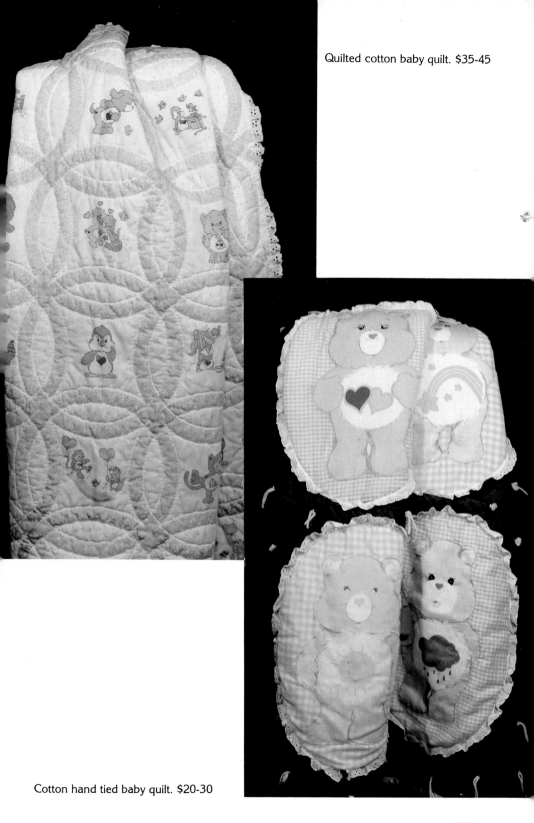

Quilted cotton baby quilt. $35-45

Cotton hand tied baby quilt. $20-30

149

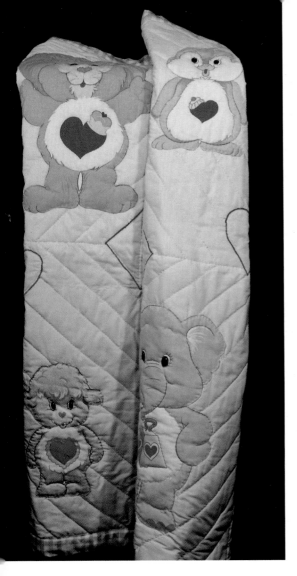

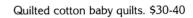
Quilted cotton baby quilts. $30-40

Cotton baby quilt. $25-35

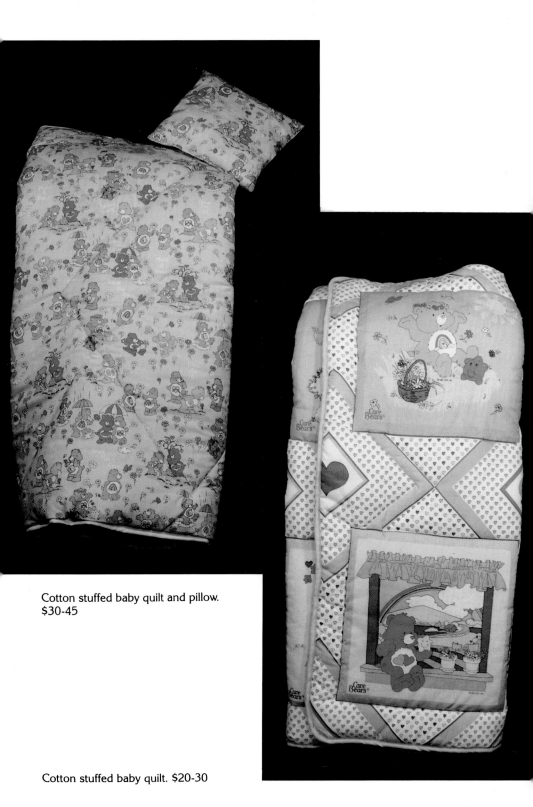

Cotton stuffed baby quilt and pillow.
$30-45

Cotton stuffed baby quilt. $20-30

151

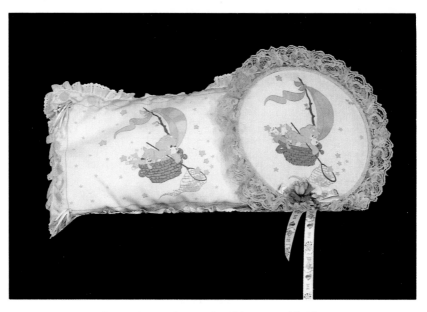

Cotton baby pillow and wall hanging. $8-10

Cotton quilted baby quilt. $30-40

Quilted baby quilts. $35-45

Cotton ruffled curtains and valance.
$20-25

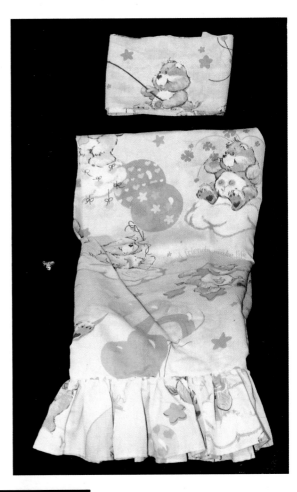

Cotton double sheet. $6-10

153

Cotton sheets and pillow case. $10-15

Cotton sheets. $6-10

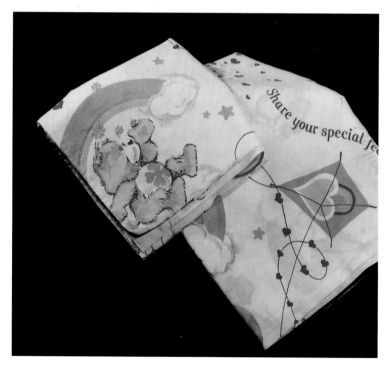

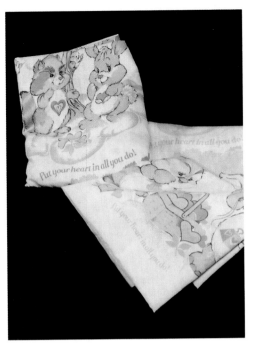

Flannel Care Bears sheet set. $15-20

Care Bears cotton pillow sham. $15-20

Care Bears cotton table cover. $25-35

Cotton baby blanket. $8-15

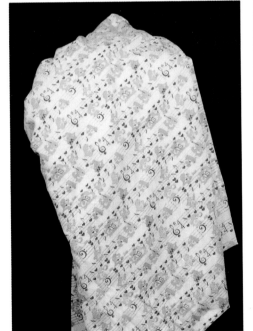

Cotton crib sheet for portable crib. $10-15

Cotton quilted blanket and receiving blanket. $20-30

Cotton baby receiving blankets. $8-15 set

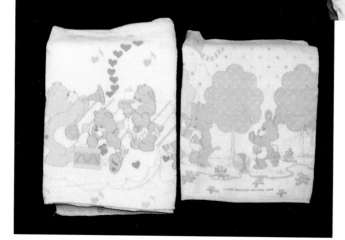

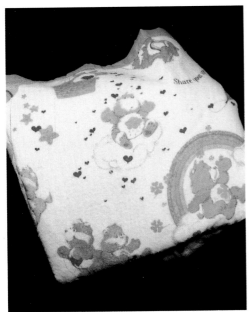

Acrylic double bed blanket. $20-30

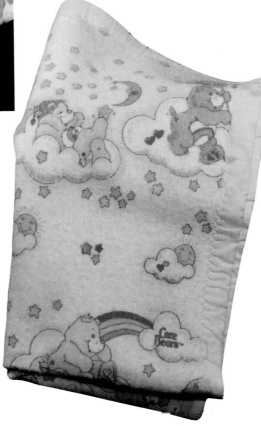

Synthetic cotton baby blanket. $20-30

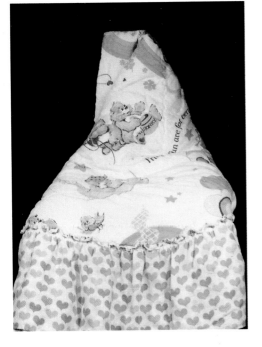

Ruffled cotton bedspread. $30-40

Cotton Funshine Bear quilt. $20-35

Nylon blend sleeping bag. $30-40

Cotton single quilt. $30-40

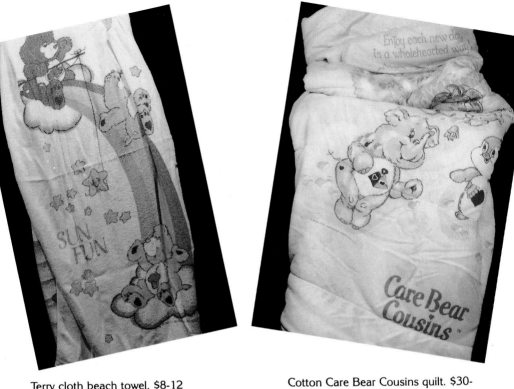

Terry cloth beach towel. $8-12

Cotton Care Bear Cousins quilt. $30-40

Cotton baby coverlet. $15-20

Cotton child's coverlet. $30-40

Terry cloth beach towel. $8-12

Terry cloth Funshine Bear beach towel. $8-12

Terry cloth bath towel. $5-8

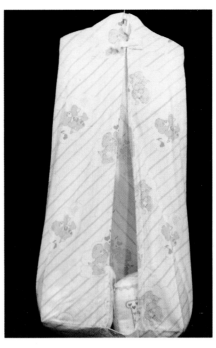

Cotton diaper holder. $6-10

Cotton diaper holder. $6-10

Cotton diaper holder. $6-10

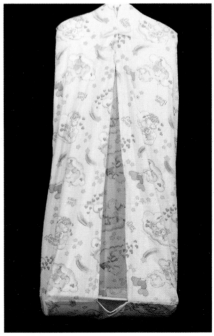

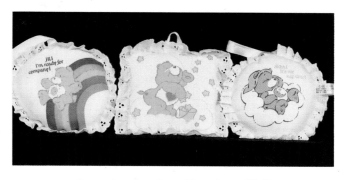

Cotton handmade wall hangings. $5-8

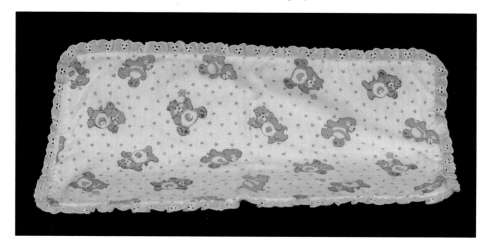

Cotton Care Bears baby bed pad.
$6-10

Cotton crib bumper. $10-15

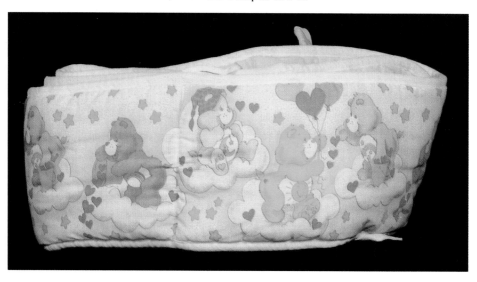

Cotton baby blocks. $8-12

Cotton baby products holder. $6-10

Cotton baby products holder. $5-10

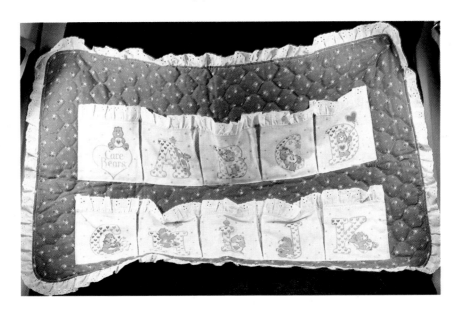

Clothes

Clothing came in polyester and cotton fabrics. Underwear, shirts, pants, skirts, pajamas, baby sleepers, as well as boy's wear all came with the Care Bears graphics and Cousins graphics.

Cotton child's tee shirt with Love-a-Lot Bear. $4-5

Cotton hooded baby shirt. $4-6

Cotton baby shirt. $3-5

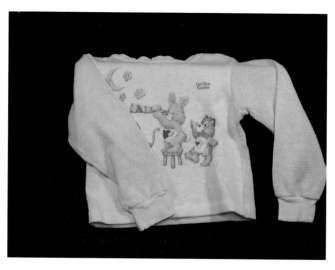

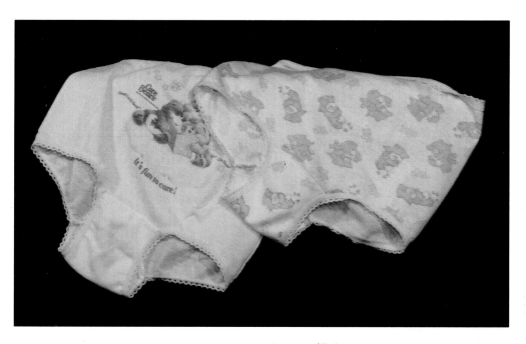

Child's cotton underwear. $3-4

Cotton baby shirt. $3-5

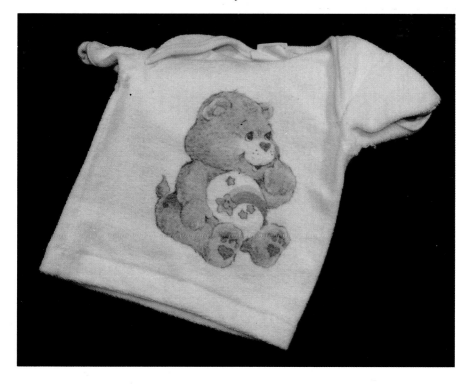

Cotton sleeveless nightie. $5-10

Cotton child's tee shirt. $3-5

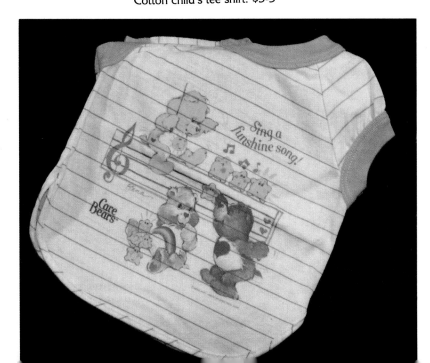

Cotton baby bunting. $15-20

Cotton child's shirt $3-5

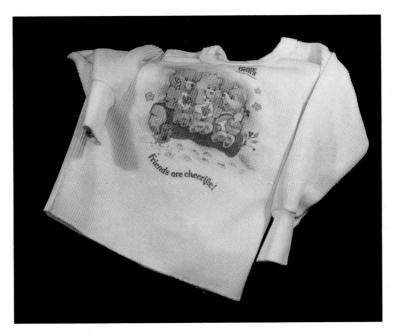

Child's cotton pajamas. $5-8

Cotton child's shirt. $3-5

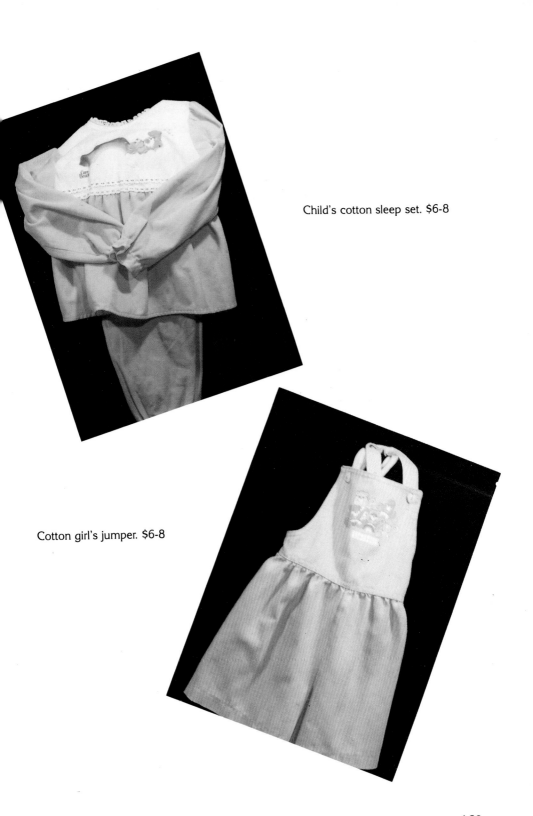

Child's cotton sleep set. $6-8

Cotton girl's jumper. $6-8

169

Nylon child's swimsuit. $5-7

Nylon child's swimsuit. $5-7

Cotton baby bonnet and baby cap. $5-7 each

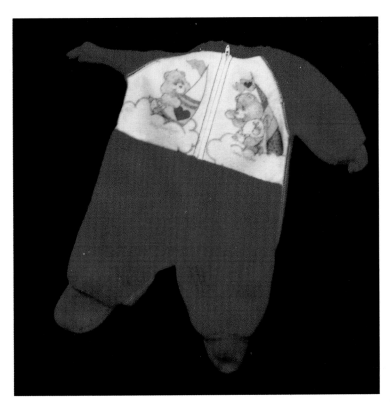

Cotton baby sleeper. $6-8

Child's cotton underwear. $3-4

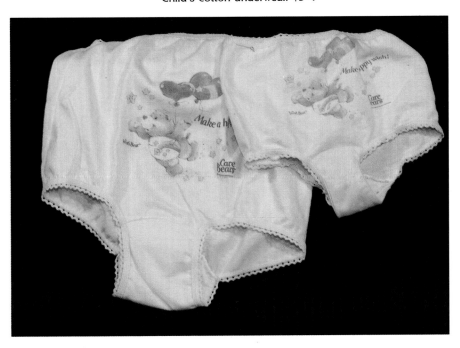

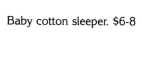

Baby cotton sleeper. $6-8

Child's cotton sleeper. $6-8

Child's cotton nightie. $6-8

Baby cotton sleeper. $5-7

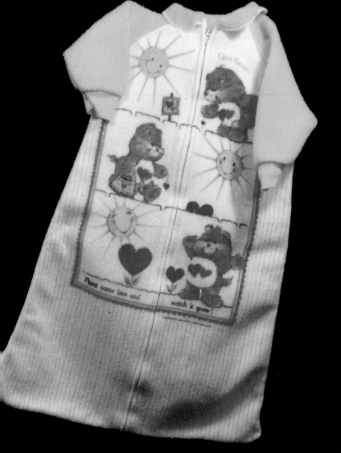

Child's cotton holiday nightie. $6-8

Cotton child's holiday nightie. $6-8

Child's cotton night gown. $6-8

Child's cotton nightie/playsuit. $5-7

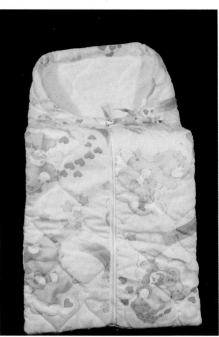

Cotton baby nightie/playsuit. $5-7

Cotton baby carrier. $4-6

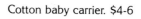

Cotton baby carrier. $4-6

Child's cotton night gown. $6-8

Cotton pre-quilted baby bibs from Paragon. $8-12 set

Cotton baby bib. $3-5

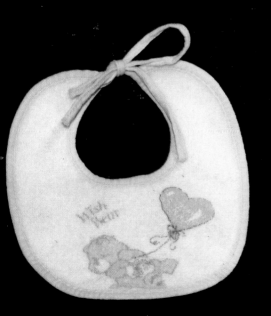

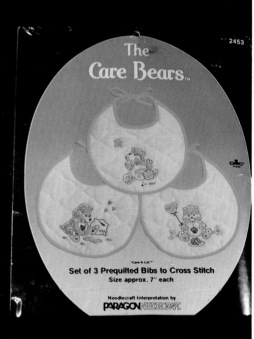

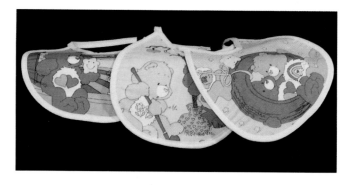

Cotton baby bibs. $4-5 each

Cotton baby bibs. $4-5 each

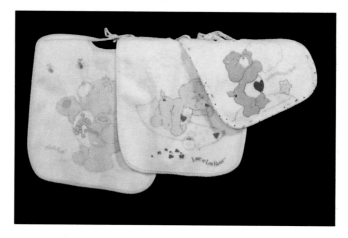

Cotton baby bonnet and booties. $10-15

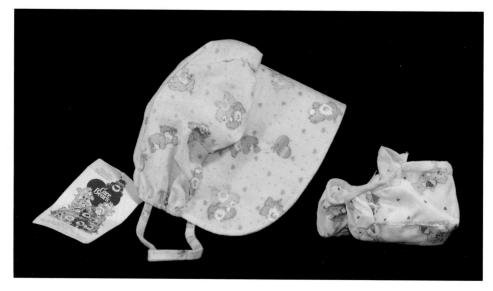

Tenderheart Bear plush slippers. $15-25

Bedtime Bear plush slippers. $15-25

Cheer Bear plush slippers. $15-25

Nylon children's mittens. $6-10

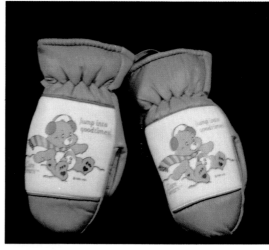

Nylon children's mittens. $6-10

Nylon children's mittens. $6-10

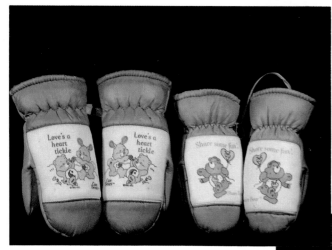

Plastic Cheer Bear and Birthday Bear
hair bands. $3-4 each

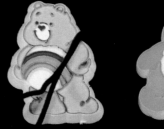

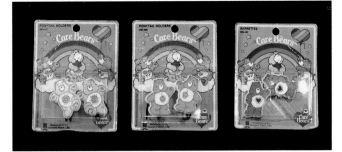

Plastic ponytail holders by Eldon Ltd. Funshine Bear, Birthday Bear, and Tenderheart Bear. $5-7 set

Plastic Birthday Bear necklace and ring. $15-20 set

Plastic Love-a-Lot Bear soap holder and comb set. $10-15

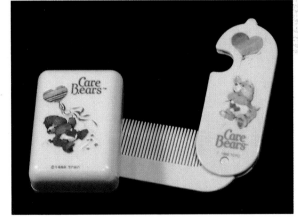

Plastic mirrors. Funshine Bear: yellow, and Cheer Bear: pink. $10-15 each

181

Care Bears barrettes. $4-5

Love-a-Lot Bear wristwatch. $40-50

Fabric Tenderheart Bear belt with metal buckle. $12-18

Plastic Care Bears child's adjustable rings. $5-8 each

Vinyl Friend Bear clothing bag in gray. $20-25

Cotton Care Bears shoe bag. $20-25

Vinyl Friend Bear clothing bag, red. $20-25

Vinyl Friend Bear clothing bag, white. $20-25

Miscellaneous

Plastic adhesive bandages. $5-8

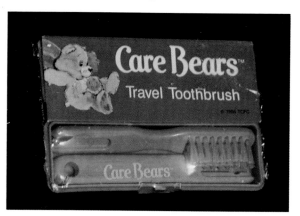

Plastic Funshine Bear toothbrush.
$10-15

Care Bears bubble bath. $4-6

Rubber Cheer Bear pencil topper. $5-8

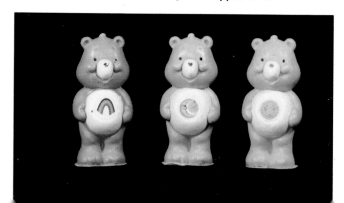

Plastic bubble bath/shampoo containers. Care Bear Cousin Lotsa Heart Elephant and Cheer Bear. $10-15

Glass Bedtime Bear candle. $10-15

Make It & Bake It sun catcher. $8-15

185

Birthday Bear and Love-a-Lot Bear candles. $8-12 each

Boxed Make It and Bake It stained glass sun catchers. $20-25

Ceramic Christmas candle holder with Good Luck Bear resting on a star. $8-15

Rubber Cheer Bear pencil topper. $5-8

186

Wax Good Luck Bear candle. $8-12 each

Wooden Wish Bear figurine. $8-12

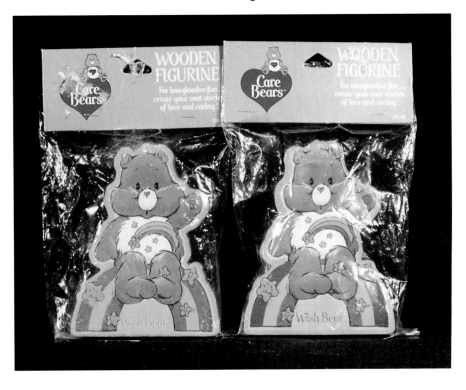

Wooden figurine of Cheer Bear. $10-15

Tenderheart Bears and Birthday Bear wooden figurines. $10-15 each

Tenderheart Bear cotton key chain. $5-8

Cheer Bear zipper pull. $6-8

Attachable zipper pulls/key chain plastic Care Bears in package. Wish Bear, Cheer Bear, and Tenderheart Bear. $8-15 each

Plastic Care Bears carrying case. $30-40

Ceramic Wish Bear Christmas ornament. 3". $15-25

Inside of vinyl Care Bears carrying case.

190

PVC Funshine and Friend Bear sitting on clouds, key chains/zipper pulls. $10-15

PVC key chains/zipper pulls. Cheer Bear, Treat Heart Pig Cousin, Friend Bear, Tenderheart Bear, and Proud Heart Cat. 1985. $8-15 each

PVC key chains/zipper pulls. Funshine Bear, Good Luck Bear, Wish Bear, Secret Heart Bear, Birthday Bear, Tenderheart Bear. 1985. $8-15 each

Plush Tenderheart Bear in original
suit. $30-40

Plastic Care Bears Wear Rainy Day
Slicker. $15-20 Available but not
shown are the Sweet Dreamers
Nightshirt and Hat, Sailor-Maid Suit
with hat to match, Sunny Swimwear
with sun glasses. All four outfits have
a special design cutout in the center
that lets the tummy symbol show
through. These outfits were sold
separately.

Bibliography:

Montgomery Ward Catalog. 1985. Chicago, Illinois.